DO YOU STILL CRY
ABOUT YOUR DEAD CAT?

ISBN-13 (print): 979-8-9877417-3-3
ISBN (ebook): 979-8-9877417-5-7

Library of Congress Control Number: 2025905926

All inquiries and requests should be addressed to the publisher.

Cover & layout design by: Rosanna Alvarez

Set in Myriad Pro

First US Edition 2025
San José, California

Published by Ocote Libre Press
www.ocotelibrepress.com

DO YOU STILL CRY

ABOUT YOUR DEAD CAT?

POETRY COLLECTION BY

JOSÉ-ARIEL CUEVAS

OCOTE LIBRE PRESS
San José, California

For my "babt,"
may each day be like our first—shiny and bright.

For my Mom,
the brightest light to have ever shown:
I am who I am because of you, and I will forever be indebted.

"Hay momentos para recitar poesías
y hay momentos para boxear."
(There's a time for reciting poems and a time for fists.)

- Roberto Bolaño,
Los Detectives Salvajes/The Savage Detectives

"Always be a poet, even in prose."

– Charles Baudelaire

"Un poeta me pidió
un consejo en el amor
En la rima me expreso
aquellas cosas de valor"

– El Manjar de los Dioses, "Un Poeta"

FOREWORD

BY ROSANNA ALVAREZ

There are books that entertain, books that inform, and then there are books that carve something raw and undeniable into your bones. *Do You Still Cry About Your Dead Cat?* is one of those books. With unflinching honesty, José-Ariel Cuevas writes from the margins—not just as an observer but as someone who has lived in the spaces often overlooked: working-class landscapes, late-night city streets, bus stops filled with people dreaming of somewhere else, and kitchen tables where love is spoken in unspoken ways.

This collection is a journey through memory and labor, love and loss, survival and reflection. Cuevas moves seamlessly between languages, between moments of tenderness and biting critique, between laughter and heartbreak. His words carry the weight of generations—of fathers who worked with calloused hands, of cities that shift and gentrify, of fleeting youth and the ghosts of what could have been.

There is a certain poetry in struggle, but too often, that poetry is romanticized from a safe distance. Cuevas does not afford himself, or the reader, that luxury. Instead, his words press into the contradictions of working-class life—the dignity and the exhaustion, the warmth of community and the alienation of long hours under fluorescent lights, the love threaded through the sharpness of a father's words. His poems and stories capture the kind of wisdom that isn't written in textbooks but is passed down through generations, exchanged in knowing glances, in a firm handshake, in the way one stands their ground in a world that often tries to erase them.

At its core, this book is about survival—not just in the physical sense, but in the way identity, history, and culture survive against the tide of assimilation, displacement, and time itself. There is an urgency here, a need to document not just personal experiences but collective truths. *Do You Still Cry About Your Dead Cat?* is a reminder that storytelling is an act of resistance, that to remember and to write is to refuse erasure.

To read this book is to recognize yourself in its pages, whether you've walked the same streets or carried a different but equally heavy inheritance. The poetry and prose here remind us that life is stitched together with contradictions: that grief and humor are often bedfellows, that working-class struggles and intellectual pursuits are not at odds, that nostalgia is both a comfort and a burden.

In a literary landscape where authenticity is often filtered and polished beyond recognition, Cuevas offers us something rare—an unapologetic, beautifully unvarnished testament to the realities of everyday life. His voice is one that refuses to be ignored, and *Do You Still Cry About Your Dead Cat?* is a book that will linger long after the last page is turned.

DO YOU
STILL CRY
ABOUT YOUR DEAD CAT?

POETRY COLLECTION BY

JOSÉ-ARIEL CUEVAS

OCOTE LIBRE PRESS
San José, California

CONTENTS

FOREWORD I

PROLOGUE 1

COFFEE WITH MY PARENTS 5

EVERY WORKDAY 6

BUSINESS AS USUAL 7

SLIVERS OF EXPOSED WINDOW PANES 8

AT FORTY-SIX 9

LABORING UNDERNEATH FLUORESCENT LIGHTS 10

REDUNDANCY 11

1983 FORD F150 WITH LANDSCAPE GEAR IN THE BED 12

THE HARVEST MOON OVER ARTEAGA, MICHOACÁN, MÉXICO 13

THE DRONING NATURE 14

TIME, IN ITS FINAL MOMENTS 15

DIONYSUS AND TRANSUBSTANTIATION 19

A COMPOSITE OF A NIGHT AT CINEBAR (RIP) 20

TIME AND THE DIVINER 22

FEIGNED ENNUI AND MANIC SHOE-GAZING 24

CINEMA VÉRITÉ 26

TIME MAKES PHILOSOPHERS OF THOSE WITH IDLE HANDS 27

ENNUI 28

Imprisoned by the Classics 29

The Divine Name 30

The Leaf's Mortality 31

A Cantankerous Deity with Plenty of Time on His Hands 32

A Haggard Angel 33

Another Faceless Monday 34

...As My Shadow Fades into the Night 35

Day to Day Existence 36

Holes in my Well-Worn Shoes 37

Fate Is That Cruel Mistress 38

I was Digging in My Left Pocket 40

Fait Accompli 41

In the World of Letters, Poetry Is the 'Hood 42

Meth and Madness, or: An Ordinary Evening
Walking Past St. James Park in Downtown San José 44

A Mexican-American Eight Grader in San José, CA 46

Awkward Teenaged Years or Halcyon Days 47

From Red to Green 48

Sub Rosa 53

On the Margins of the Margin 54

Providence Guided by My Own Hand 56

The Past, Heavily-Filtered 58

I Follow Her Specter 59

In All Her Libertine Glory 60

Nihilism Kills the Optimist 61

Shelter in a Paper House 62

Lust is in the Air 63

The Furthest Things from Me 64

The Nihilist Rhapsodizes 65

Sweet Lady Añejo: a Valentine 69

The Consoler in Search of a Sympathetic Ear

(or: A Flickering Light and an Unmade, Twin-Sized Bed) 70

A Siren Song and its Insurmountable Distance 72

Refraction 73

Solipsistic 74

In Vice, I Thrust Myself 76

Life, Lust, Death and the Smiths 77

My Other Shoe 81

Living in a City Named After a Saint 82

In This Glorified Suburb 84

Contemplations and Trivial Pursuits 86

Like an Ebbing Tide 88

Christ-Hustlers and Pleasure-Seekers 90

We Walk Along the Gutter 91

We Run Like Thieves 92

…His Pale Horse Gallops Slowly 93

A Meditation on Death (RIP Abuelita María) 94

Life (as Lived through Pulp's "Common People") 97

Wax Rhapsodic 98

That Is Why We Sing the Songs That We Do 100

I Am That Piece of Creased Paper 102

"Alternaverse" 104

Alas (Another Day Has Started) 106

Roberto Bolaño 109

The Shaky Convictions of the Easily Amused 110

Acknowledgments. 115

About the Author. 117

PROLOGUE

There is what you learn in an academic setting, and what you learn living life as the son of immigrants. The most informative texts cannot prepare you for the most insightful, piercing, sobering words of wisdom borne from generations of lives lived in the soil and mountains of Arteaga, Michoacán de Ocampo, México. Monosyllabic words that got you pegged from a mile away, they see through you and give you no time to put on pretenses. My Dad comes from that lineage of stoic men who gave little in emotions, but plenty when it came to stern guidance that one chose to follow or not. It was far from perfect, and often times fraught with tension. But as time went on and he got older and so did I, he mellowed out some, and I became more understanding of what he went through, how he was reared, and how that transferred onto us. It was quite the path taken to one of the avenues it led to—me, with my partner, sitting at my parents' kitchen table, talking, drinking coffee, when unprompted, he asks me, "So, do you still cry about your dead cat?"

COFFEE WITH MY PARENTS

There is this bluntness with an undertone of cruelty that,
though unintended, can sting you mightily,
cut you to the bone and field dress you.
It is a left hook hidden behind a right,
probing jab that momentarily separates you
from your senses.

I was sitting at my parents' dinner table,
with my partner by my side,
and in between sips of Don Francisco Instant Coffee,
my Dad asks me, flatly, "Do you still cry about your dead cat?"
Stunned, all I could muster were nonsensical monosyllabic replies,
independent of one another.

Cats hold this place in my heart
that dogs will always be just barely on the other side of—
and I say this as someone who has had dogs for pets
and loved them to the moon and back.

Something about a feline finally deeming you worthy
of their indifference as you shower them
with adulation that speaks to me.
They are like those hipsters from the early 2000's
that treated small-scale concerts like art exhibits—
standing still, stroking one's chin, giving pithy remarks
while drinking a rapidly-warming Pabst Blue Ribbon.

Cats might as well have been riding around
in a comically small fixed-gear bicycle
with how cool and disaffected they can be.
I felt like I joined an exclusive club
the moment Pearl deemed me head-bunting worthy.

EVERY WORKDAY

Every workday
I walk 35,000 steps,
Lapping the premises
Many times over.
That is over seventeen miles
Of worn feet,
Of shins slowly splintering.
Seventeen miles of existential doldrums
In constant loop.
There are days when things run smoothly,
then there are days
where you are pulled taut,
every bit of fiber struggling
to maintain their integrity.
It is yeoman's work
without a cause nor glory,
but plenty of exhaustion
and pulled muscles.
At the bar,
I throw back a shot:
Here's to the faceless cogs
That keep the machine humming.
To the people whose names are secondary,
Gripping life with their calloused hands.

BUSINESS AS USUAL

The owner of the casino I worked at
passed away on April 8th, 2019.
He was a nice man,
but a capitalist to the core.
He kept wages down
(below market rate);
he kept us poor,
but not poor enough
to qualify for public assistance.
Living on credit and borrowed time,
I would peruse the classifieds,
shaking off years of fear and subservience,
because while the owner
shed his mortal coil,
his son has taken over,
and it was business as usual.
Like an Ebbing Tide

SLIVERS OF EXPOSED WINDOW PANES

The Calendar says it's Tuesday,
but physically,
it is Sunday,
it is My Sunday.
I am sitting at a craft beer pub;
it is a type of place
where children and pets are permitted.
I am here,
nursing an imperial stout,
watching life pass me by
through the slivers of exposed windowpanes.
People wander through,
stumble out,
amble by,
or whiz past
in one of those obnoxious rental scooters.
The crowd ebbs and flows
while my snifter is slowly imbibed.
I could go for some whiskey,
but this bar is beer only.
> *Ah, I find myself at the crossroads yet again.*
> > I reach for my moleskin journal,
> > opening it to the next blank page,
> > pondering what to write about next.

At Forty-Six

After you reach the age of forty-six,
your friends are less likely to die
vía homicide
as they are by suicide
or illness.
That is the open door
you seldom want
to go through.

Laboring Underneath Fluorescent Lights

Your body breaking down
at such a young age
is the tribute paid
to the altar
of the invisible hand
of the free market.
It feeds on your
economic anxieties
and bathes in blood
drained from every single
one of your pores.
Right to work
is the right to work you
until you shed your mortal coil
while laboring underneath fluorescent lights.

REDUNDANCY

It is a day,
another day
that ends in Y.
Sans character,
they bleed into each other.
Youthful locks have given way to
grey hairs and rent-anxiety.
No more *joie de vivre*,
but lots of "chingas,
o te chingan"

1983 FORD F150 WITH LANDSCAPE GEAR IN THE BED

Every workday, the alarm goes off at 6:30 a.m.,
and I commence with the morning ritual:
I get up, I make breakfast for me and my partner,
I wish her well as she walks out the door,
and I measure the remaining free time
to see if I have time to prepare my lunch and to workout.
The alarm on my phone is a pleasant one
("Homecoming" is the name Samsung gave this melody);
 it is much nicer than the one associated with
the alarm I used for my previous job,
which was a soundtrack to a death march.
Sometimes I wish my phone had a
"1983 Ford F150 with Landscape Gear in the Bed"
alarm sound to serenade me
with the morning sounds of East Side San José.
It is a metronome that has my internal clock finely tuned.
Maybe I am regressing, or am in a static state
of arrested development,
but when my mind conjures up that sound
and plays it in a constant loop,
I start to feel warm, as if it were a San Marcos blanket
(brown-on-tan, with a lion or a tiger print)
and I am ensconced in its polyester fabrics,
as it lessens the burden of the weight of the world.

THE HARVEST MOON OVER ARTEAGA, MICHOACÁN, MÉXICO

Standing beneath the harvest moon,
hand over heart,
clutching a sun-beaten straw hat.
My huaraches, covered
with the same earth that has given
so much over the years.

THE DRONING NATURE

My body hurts from the punches
life is throwing.
An onslaught of haymakers
are trying to finish off
what work with little reward have done…
and are doing.
Hands are lightly calloused,
but my soul is buried in scar tissue
and my feet…
those dogs are barking.
I drink some coffee
from a place I tend to frequent
when the sun starts to descend.
Rather than finding my center,
my jaded conscience
is now trafficking in unfiltered thoughts
and unfettered stream-of-conscience
internal dialogue
(when not chain-smoking.)
There is a line in The Old Man and the Sea that goes:
"A man is not made for defeat…
a man can be destroyed but not defeated."
Then, I remembered
that Ernest Hemingway took his own life.
Tomorrow is payday,
which for a moment,
lessens the pain of life's punches.

Time, In Its Final Moments

It's almost a tragedy
When I see all the time
I have in the world
Slowly die as each second
Grabs a hold of the skin
On my hands,
Searching for comfort
In their final moments.
I sing them a song of comfort,
One passed down through
Generation after generation
Of Caballero women
In the rustic landscape
Of Michoacán,
To ease their transition
From present to past tense.

DIONYSUS AND TRANSUBSTANTIATION

Sun-kissed days outside Matisse—
you with a blonde Caesar hairdo
and a story to tell,
me, with a Djarum firmly pressed
between my index and middle finger,
and a sympathetic ear.
We talked about Dionysus and transubstantiation,
about Smashing Pumpkins versus Pavement,
about which band playing at Cactus
was worth watching.
Years later, with graying temples,
and in between drags of an American Spirit menthol,
I wonder where time went,
I wonder where you went as well.

A Composite of a Night at Cinebar (RIP)

As I stand outside Cinebar,
 smoking a cigarette,
watching cars stalled on San Fernando Street,
 I wonder if I am the wastetoid
example mothers point out to their kids.
Their stares are cold enough
to cool a Summer's day;
judging blindly,
while my smoke drifts away.
In their faces,
I see time slipping by,
oozing from my fingers
and into the void.
In my reflection,
I see my youth has absconded,
and in its place,
a graying husk,
a reminder that time
is fickle and fleeing.
My halcyon days
were brief,
a flash in the evening sky
that would soon swallow
and envelop it in its darkness.
My present is covered
in calloused skin
and scar tissue,
while intellectual pursuits
have become more

of a luxury
than a leisurely pursuit.
The sun is perched
on South 4th street,
while ashes fall on my hand,
and my beer, getting warmer
as I get older.

Joel Friström
Dec. 30th 1979 - Aug. 22nd 2017

Time and the Diviner

What is tomorrow if not a broken
promise waiting to happen?
Perhaps it is an excuse to daydream,
forgetting that the ground is shifting beneath you
as time marches on while you're standing still-
eyes squinted, hands in pocket, mind adrift.

How can the future be what you make of it,
if all you do is dream of it and its possible outcome?
Thoughts of love and prosperity consume you,
all the while your train came and went,
leaving you to stand next to an evangelic
who wants your time and your stranger of a soul.

(He asks, "Do you know what awaits you in the next life?"
Your reply, "Sometimes I don't even know my own name,
let alone what is waiting for me in the hereafter.")

Tomorrow is a luxurious concept,
as unreliable as public transportation.
Reflective… not philosophically,
but in a hall-of-mirrors sort of way.
Anxiously you look for the next train;
it feels as if you've been waiting for eighteen hours.

Eighteen hours or a lifetime:
Tomorrow is starting to resemble your nameless girlfriend,
the one who broke more promises
than nineteenth century heads of state.
The one who is more myth than human,
as her memory lasted longer than her time in your life.

You feel like you've been had,
hoodwinked by some shiftless diviner
who manipulated time to forecast your future,
all the while your pockets were turned inside out,
taking both your money and your remaining shred of dignity...
and the train, it still hasn't come yet.
taking both your money and your remaining shred of dignity...
and the train, it still hasn't come yet.

FEIGNED ENNUI AND MANIC SHOE-GAZING

Cigarette smolders between
my index and middle fingers,
lit…the smoke wafts in the air,
dancing a carcinogenic fandango.
I catch it from time to time,
in between bouts of feigned ennui
and manic shoe-gazing.
I fumble for my phone,
only to resent its silence,
as the world hums
and hides behind its silhouette.
The lights of the intersection
trade off each other-
red for green, green for red-
while I stand alone,
save for the slow-burning
pure tobacco cigarette
I occasionally draw smoke from.
The soft glow from the cherry
is my companion by default.
Lovers walk past,
fingers locked,
zigzagging,
riding the wave
of lust and vino.
In the opposite direction,
a crowd of silver-haired conventioneers
amble and hustle
to the nearest gastro pub.
In this bustle,

I stand like a touchstone,
or some other
easily-ignored totem.
It is the same play,
over and over,
and I watch it
with the enthusiasm
of a jaded patron.
War is hell—
whether it's on a battlefield,
or within as you cross paths
with the object of your affection
as she makes her way
with someone who isn't you.
My stoic look gives way
to the anguish I felt inside,
as soon as she was long gone.
With a flick of my Zippo,
another cigarette is lit.
With plenty of time still on my hands,
I ruminate over seeing a living phantasm.
"Love is a fantasy,"
I murmur to myself,
perhaps to the rose vendor
who walked past me
a couple of minutes ago.
Perhaps, I said it to myself,
one final volley
as inertia slowly
gives way to atrophy.

Cinema Vérité

Life before my eyes
unfolds like a cinema
of the absurd
and (self-)absorbed.

The plot lines seem
jagged and crooked,
as if the city has given up
spending on its infrastructure.

Love is born, and then it dies,
all the while,
traffic lights turn greed to red, to green again
(life goes on, whether you want it to or not.)

I observe all this,
self-conscious of
being a bad actor
in someone else's movie.

TIME MAKES PHILOSOPHERS OF THOSE WITH IDLE HANDS

Sitting with a three-dollar coffee
in what was once a red-light district,

a dog-eared, well-worn
copy of The Idiot
is my faithful companion.

I think of loves that have burned brightly,
and flickered dimly.

Time makes philosophers
of those with idle hands
and slowly-cooling coffee cups.

ENNUI

Walking downtown,
eyes half-focused on the
ground—
what's in front,
what's left behind.
What's in front?
Dull gray slabs
of city pavement
partially covered in detritus,
partially nude.

A constellation of faces
rush forward and drift away.
It is rush hour,
no matter the time.
The overcast sky
crashes onto the sides
of half-assed office buildings.

It's gray-on-gray violence,
a waltz of monotony
broken by some graffiti here
and some faded flyers there.
Near the corner,
a barren tree stands still,
withered, dampened leaves
surround it,
like the slip of a drunken lady
who clumsily stripped herself
using only her calloused feet.

Music app shuffling
between Nick Drake
and Dirty Beaches'
last album,
a fitting soundtrack
to my own shuffle.

What I left behind
and what's in front
is a dull, gray void—
only my pockets
are emptier.

Imprisoned by the Classics

Imprisoned by the classics,
in bars made of metered words
and stanzas stilted and stale.
These books of influence
are dusty sarcophagi
to various schools of thought
now shuttered and retired.
The sun has set on the old,
and the new has yet to rise.
Meanwhile, I rattle my cup
over these musty rails,
waiting on the warden
to bring me a new book.

THE DIVINE NAME

There are no Atheists in the foxhole,
or so the saying goes.
As for a hospital,
I do not know if there are any,
or if they're at a parking lot,
drinking cafeteria coffee,
smoking cigarettes,
gloomily watching
as the ashes rain onto the asphalt.
They look at a loved one
wrestling with destiny's inevitability,
dancing with acceptance and denial.
In a moment of crisis, or duress,
we take Pascal's wager—
the divine name silently
drips off our lips.

THE LEAF'S MORTALITY

Another year,
another batch of leaves
on the floor,
losing color,
dying.
Dying on the pavement,
forgotten, anonymous.
Its halcyon days
have long since passed.
Its autumn death is cold,
mechanical—it is a ritual.
The leaf's mortality
fucks with my mind,
as I sit and watch, smoking
while I ponder this lost year.

A CANTANKEROUS DEITY WITH PLENTY OF TIME ON HIS HANDS

Nostalgia: A rosy picture
painted by a mind
dealing with the inevitability
that the present didn't unfold
as previously planned.
That all we are
are just grains of sand
sinking down the hourglass,
thrust downward by other granule realizations
that their dreams are stillbirth.
Perhaps that explains
why every step I take
feels heavy, or as if
I am trudging through a bed of
quick-drying cement.
Some might say that the future
is a blank slate,
that there is plenty of time
to dictate how
things end up.
But I trudge along,
weary, worried
that my slate is being filled
by a cantankerous deity
with plenty of time on his hands.

A HAGGARD ANGEL

A haggard angel,
with dirt-encrusted wings,
sits beside me,
and asks me for a cigarette.
Her halo, askew,
teeters on the edge,
gently kissing her right ear.
Dark circles underneath her eyes,
she contemplates life, as she sits here,
hypnotized by the smoke
dancing a fandango in mid-air.
She speaks only in past tenses,
about who she was in her better days.
She is like one of Kerouac's mad ones,
a star that shone brightly,
and burned out before her time.

ANOTHER FACELESS MONDAY

I sit outside a café,
it is a perfect day to pursue
Bohemian pleasures.
I light a cigarette,
and sip my coffee,
while I contemplate
the book that lies there in front of me—
edges bent, chipped pine,
and pages filled of poetry
written by the greats of Latin America.
My eyes suddenly drift to the chair on my left
(slightly past that chair, are two women
with matching phones, and matching tastes
for Marlboro Lights),
then my right
(A singer/songwriter with an acoustic guitar
serenading his beloved with a sweet song
vía Zoom—with choppy reception)…
I am reminded that I am flanked by solitude.
Although there are people abound,
and hobos occasionally stop to bum cigarettes from me,
and the café worker smiles
as she buses the dirty dishes,
I remain alone.

...As My Shadow Fades into the Night

The moon hangs still, distant,
looking at us from above,
from behind wispy clouds,
ebbing and flowing like nocturnal tides.
I stare at it from the uneven pavement
that constitutes my station in life.
The air breezes past,
carrying with it the bitter taste
of a city marching forward.
I hear faint, manic echoes
coming from all points,
but all I see is my shadow
projected on this dull,
grey stucco wall.
I stand here, hands in pocket,
my lunar-gazing eyes still sky-bound,
My left foot straddles the pavement,
as I dig for a cigarette.
I dug out my crushed box,
holding my last, crooked cigarette
(more crooked than my smile.)
The lights are getting dimmer,
my breathing gets increasingly shallow
as my shadow fades into the night.

DAY TO DAY EXISTENCE

I was born *in* the bottom.
I live *in* the bottom.
How long will I survive?
As long as my uninsured,
addled-with-all-that-might-kill-me
body allows me to.
This is not an ode to the downtrodden,
or a valentine to the hardscrabble,
working class life.
It is a simple declaration
of where I am.
Potential is the fruit
rotting on the branches
of a tree far from my reach.
I see it when I go to work.
I see it when I'm not called in to go to work.
I see it when I sigh in despair,
and when I smile in recognition
of what I have
(which still is more than others.)

Holes in my Well-Worn Shoes

I walk around with my back slightly hunched,
like a beast of burden
with impish devils on either shoulder,
poking, prodding, looking for the button
that controls my baser instincts.
The miles I have walked are measured
by the holes in my well-worn shoes,
and the grey hairs that are creeping up
like the seasons of despair.
The sun is at a distance,
the road is crooked,
and the burden,
on my back like a first-class passenger.

Fate Is That Cruel Mistress

Some people love tempting fate.
They chase it like the ultimate high
they felt when they smoked marijuana
for the first time in their lives.
More often than not,
those souls longing for her touch
are left behind in a cloud of dust
and dejection.
There are a few who have met her
face to face—
feeling the sweet caress of her left hand,
while her right swings
a freshly-sharpened scythe.
She swings it slowly,
without warning.
Slow enough to see it coming,
slow enough to question
whether or not you want
to get out of the way.
Fate is that cruel mistress
people have written about.
We've been warned,
yet here we are,
talking about her sweet song of seduction.
She beckons you from the other side,
using her delicate finger
to motion to you to come,
to crash into her heaving bosom,
to taste the sweetness of her kiss,

and the wild nights foreshadowed
by her love bites.
When she's gone, she's gone for good,
taking with her her midnight black shawl,
a crimson-lined scythe,
and what is now the former "you".
What's left are memories
of those wild times
where we stared off into the infinite west
and wondered about life, love, poetry,
and whether the future would be kinder
than the fucked-up present.

I was Digging in My Left Pocket...

I was digging in my left pocket for my Zippo.
It was a deep dig.
A lady lawyer, walking past,
thought I was pleasuring myself.
All of this happened in an alleyway,
separating South Second and South First Streets
in downtown San José.
In a way, her reaction was just:
piss-soaked alley;
she, trying to get to her office;
I, looking sick, disheveled,
mucus-encrusted nose,
cigarette dangling from my mouth,
wanting to be lit,
digging through my pocket
like a junky looking for that one penny he picked up,
and the pleasurable sigh when I found
the intended object.

FAIT ACCOMPLI

On the surface,
life seems to be a series
of random occurrences
crashing into each other
(chaos trapped in flesh and bones,
wrapped in skin that has seen better days.)
Mistakes and regrets
are cleaned up
and passed off as "learning experiences".
That is what one does
to maintain self control—
a flimsy façade.
More than likely,
life is more like a casino,
where the house usually wins
and you hope to break even.
Yeah, a rigged parlor game
where you are fucked no matter what.

In the World of Letters, Poetry Is the 'Hood

I traffic in poetry,
and in the world of letters,
poetry is the 'hood:
the east side of town,
the other side of the tracks,
the urine-soaked alleys
of downtown nowhere.
Storm drains are clogged
with printed-out dead-ends
and rejected manuscripts.
The moon hangs at a distance,
its reflection of sunlight
resembles half-burnt out
neon signs of ghost town taquerías
and hourly rate motels
that dot this cityscape.
Dive bars are a dime-a-dozen,
where soused Bukowskis
drink side-by-side with debauched Baudelaires,
and a dead-end Kerouac
ruminates over the choices he has made,
while his stool neighbor, Bolaño,
orders another Negra Modelo.
Ginsberg stands alone outside,
reciting some lines he just wrote,
while cigarette smoke wafts around,
draping his syllables with nicotine and menthol.
Octavio Paz walks by,
dressed and looking
like a powerful hacienda owner,

and gives a look of disgust
at this bearded homosexual
spouting stream of consciousness thoughts.
He has no time to listen,
for he will see what he once was,
and he has no time for that.
"Last CALL!" shouts the bartender.
The denizens of this free-verse ghetto
shuffle, amble their way out;
their eyes drift northward,
to a distant moon
shrouded by drifting clouds.
They all walk to that taquería,
turning a ghost town
into a city full of mumbling life
(semi-drowned out by the buzzing neon sign.)

METH AND MADNESS, OR: AN ORDINARY EVENING WALKING PAST ST. JAMES PARK IN DOWNTOWN SAN JOSÉ

The evening rages on,
like a kegger along fraternity row
near San José State University.
Well, the sun barely went down,
but the lunatic parade at the first hint of nightfall
makes it feel everlasting.
Meth and madness,
or: an ordinary evening
walking past St. James Park
in downtown San José.
The wind reverberates all along South First Street—
sounding sad, distant, discordant.
Bus after bus whistle past…
faces beaten up by life,
kicked by consequences,
spat upon by reality
adorn these windows,
while hipsters and modern-day hippies
drink barley wine at a vegan shop,
smoking from hand-rolled cigarettes.
mingle with hipster-y talk
Bros and bros with ties
stumble out of a craft brew pub,
burning off Dunhill Lights and regaling
each other with their tales of conquest
and who has the largest expense account
(everything is a pissing contest with them.)
The evening rages on,
howling like a feral wolf,

or like the warbling
of the typical racist on Twitter.
I walk past it all
with a mind burdened by
my own tribulations,
dulled by moderately-priced beer,
piqued by natural, menthol cigarettes,
bummed by the current feeling
of being a man without a flag,
or a sympathetic ear
(beyond my circle of friends.)
It's 9:37pm,
I am making my way to the bus stop.
My heart has nobody to beat for,
however, time is my current master.

A Mexican-American Eighth Grader in San José, CA

1992:
It was my final year
at Fischer Middle School.
The disco revival
was in its ascendancy.
Vans were also making a return
to the national consciousness.
Dr. Dre was about to drop "The Chronic",
ushering in the G-Funk era.

Everywhere and nowhere:
I was not a gangster
and I was far from being a pretty-boy.
I was just a Mexican kid with curly hair
who would be confused for being Samoan, or Tongan.

Awkward Teenaged Years or Halcyon Days

The beer in the glass goes counter-clockwise
as I swirl and swirl it some more.
I scratch the side of the pint glass,
peeling the imaginary label
off of the Guinness I am drinking.
My mind drifts past the shiftless drifters
drinking cans of Olympia and cheap scotch
and the tattooed Camel Wides-smoking indie rock priestess.
It goes further back, back into time,
and without stopping anywhere,
my mind drifts back.
Putting away the beer and stepping out for a cigarette,
I begin to wonder if my awkward teenaged years
were also my halcyon days.

From Red to Green

Time spans further than memory,
and whatever is within reach
is muddied by what is projected.
Reality is substituted for a myth
constructed despite the perils
transpiring in this waking life.
With eyes shut,
a tinseled wonderland appears
from beneath the oil-stained asphalt.
Instead of mad-hatters and caterpillars,
there is a scantily-clad woman
and earthly delights aplenty.
Without knowing, the lights went from red to green,
all that you've ever cherished has passed you by;
your eyes remain shut and your grin
                              … sheepish.

Sub Rosa

In the cover of night,
away from prying eyes,
stares are stolen,
love is made,
while the moon and stars
pledge an oath of silence

ON THE MARGINS OF THE MARGIN

She was twenty-three
when I met her by chance
(drinking Jack and ginger,
with eyes as dead as the evening.)

I said "hello",
but those words echoed through her ears.
She focused on her drink,
stirring it, hoping for something.

I ordered a Maker's Mark neat,
sipped a couple of casual sips,
put a coaster on my tumbler,
and stepped outside for a smoke.

She stepped outside and asked for a cigarette—
we talked about Oakland A's baseball,
about how life is hard when you're born
with your back already against the wall.

Her neckline dipped a little bit,
into a valley of light, cinnamon flesh.
It wasn't a full-on exhibition,
but a man could get an idea of what she's working with.

Her body is a road map
of scars and varicose veins.
A temple of bruises
and debauched sensibilities.

I went inside to tend to my neglected drink,
leaving her to her own devices,
while I tended to mine.

San José is something
when you're on the margins
of the margin.

PROVIDENCE GUIDED BY MY OWN HAND

It is the Tuesday after Memorial Day, Which means that the university, the community colleges, and most high schools have had their graduation ceremonies. The bus wasn't as packed, but it went at a leisurely pace… as always. There are a few more seats available, from now until the start of summer session. But for now, there are seats available. I can avoid sitting on the bench seats, avoid the uncomfortable eye contact with the lady who has as many bags in her possession as she has underneath her sleep-deprived eyes. I sit in the back, on the left-hand side, staring out the window, watching cars zoom past. I briefly think about the Montgomery bus boycotts, about what Rosa Parks and others went through, and the fruit of the boycotters' labor are…my choice to sit at the very back. My mind soon drifts to my music, to what strain of indie rock I should listen to: lo-fi, or synth-driven music? I can be fickle at times, but it's just that with each minute I spend staring out the window, my mind more and more starts to resemble a short-attention span film festival. Here's my stop; I ring the bell accordingly.

I now find myself downtown, my feet (and to a certain extent, my liver) are feeling restless—as restless as the motorists that are, unbeknownst to them, serenading me with their bleating horns. I make my way through these familiar streets; the wind gently kisses me with its polluted essence. I pass by the hotels and bank buildings. I pass by vacant storefronts; now there seems to be more and more—dotting the landscape like unmarked headstones in a pauper's cemetery. Rush…rush go the people, some with security badges, and some with county hospital wristbands. They rush past the guy standing on the brim of Paseo de San Antonio, playing his saxophone (a Charlie Parker number, if I'm not mistaken); they rush past the old Asian lady who is on no one's time but her own. Their destination is unknown to me, but my short-term destiny has manifested itself in the form of my favorite café.

I find myself a patio table on the outside-a chipped, tiled table with

56

a wobbly leg-where I lay my book and rest my pint glass. I take the first sip of a freshly-poured stout, and for some reason, I heard the opening line to Etta James'"At Last". I have had this particular beer many times before, but the first drink always makes me feel like a divine being drinking a chalice full of ambrosia. I then light a cigarette; it complements the beer as much as a glove does to a hand. I stare at the spine of the book I am toting along—it is a magical realism tome that could only have been written by Latin American authors of a certain vintage. I take another sip of my beer, I swirl it a bit, and stare at the head—how it clings to the side of the glass as the rest slowly settles, resembling a rich, lush coffee. I stare at the spine again, though literature is not what is calling me at this moment. That one question that dances in my head is back again— is it destiny, or is it a random occurrence where we end up?

Philosophy has always been an interest of mine, whether I fully understand the philosopher's intent, or if my comprehension was skin deep at best. Whatever it is that you might be feeling, there will be a pearl of wisdom written by some guy who died a couple of hundred years ago. Love, angst, dread, irony, or a simple question of "why", it is out there. There are many schools of logic out in the wild. More often than not, different schools of philosophy clash like rival gangs dressed in tweed jackets with leather patches on the elbows.

Summer is slowly creeping in (and I, as well, am tired of the silly games), and romance hangs in the air. At the moment, the only thing I'm romancing is this pint that's nearly done. My eyes drift back to the spine, and if there is one thing that I've learned from reading Gabriel García-Márquez is that, to be patient, and what will come will come. (Providence guided by my own hand.) So, I guess it's all a matter of time—something that I have in abundance. And if there is one thing that I know for sure, it's that I have the patience of a caffeine-addled, nicotine-addicted saint with jittery hands.

THE PAST, HEAVILY-FILTERED

The smell of Coco Chanel
hangs in the air.
Slowly, it begins to drift,
dancing seductively,
teasing me with its
aromatic beauty.
It is a familiar scent,
though the host
is a different vessel.
The one I remember,
she was a tapestry
of European elegance
and indigenous beauty,
with features as delicate
as a porcelain doll.
She had a penchant
for pilsners and lagers,
for Patrón and red wine.
I turn and turn,
staring madly at the crowd,
trying hard to see
if the past is on the verge
of being reborn.
I stand in the middle
of the pavement,
my nose, trying to track
the scent that is slowly fading
into the brisk air
of an early summer day
in San José, California.

Empty-handed,
empty-heart,
I start walking somewhere,
anywhere that is not here.
No matter where I am at,
the past, heavily-filtered,
is there, haunting me
with its rose-tinted,
five foot, three inch specter.

I Follow Her Specter

The urge to fuck is strong,
Like a thousand searing needles
Shooting instant death
Through the veins
Of transients meandering
Outside of the Greyhound bus station
In downtown Los Angeles.
Angling for a fix,
They do what they can;
I do what I can to fill the void
By twisting and turning
In the vapors of the whiskey
I am currently drinking,
Fancying it to be the innards
Of the faceless woman I desire.
I follow her specter from bar to bar,
Collapsing in the gutter,
My hands always beyond her reach.
A friend of mine finds me there
Muttering incoherently.
He lifts me up and asks if I was okay,
All I could say was the title of that Stone Roses song,
"I wanna be adored".

In All Her Libertine Glory

She cuts me with her razor lips;
blood drips from my cheek,
leaving an indecipherable,
crimson-colored Rorschach pattern
on my shirt.
 She stands at a distance like Venus—
nude, in all her libertine glory.
My hands reach for her,
but all they grasp are air
and a fleeting sense of euphoria.
There was no afterglow,
only cigarette smoke and the feeling
of being the protagonist
of every single jilted-lover poem
ever written.

NIHILISM KILLS THE OPTIMIST

My heavily scribbled notebook is full of
fragmented stanzas, unrequited overtures
and Valentine's long past their sell-by date.
No methods, slight madness,
some Es before Is,
and some long-absent Us.
Words without reason
are corralled in a ring of coffee
with cigarette ash-stained barbed wire.
There is a line that started in the Fall
and sputtered along on wobbly legs
to the first week of Winter.
From ecstasy and abstract optimism,
to despair and resignation—
nihilism kills the optimist.
Friend Zone: a barren wasteland
with overly-delineated borders
adorned with silver medals and runner-up trophies.
That's where love dies a humble death,
slowly decomposing in a coffin
of thin, college ruled paper.

Shelter in a Paper House

The rain is for lovers
and lovers of misery.
Couples are drawn to the beat
of each other's heart.
Striding hand-in-hand,
they romp through the puddles,
laughing and playing with a shared innocence
that hides both the carnal, urgent desire
and tribulations of the previous day.
On the other side of the misty café window,
solitary figures walk past,
stopping every now and again to curse the rain.
They look inward for sanctuary,
only to find their minds cluttered
with decaying ideas and wistful nostalgia.
(It is as useful as finding shelter in a paper house.)
For some, the rain is nature's mirror
that reflects the youthful ecstasy
that burns deep within.
For others, it is a form of torture
that Torquemada himself
could never imagine.

LUST IS IN THE AIR

It's a cold night,
the wind feels like an infinite set of needles
poking at every single pore of my body.
It's a perfect moment for a jacket,
but I've been out all day
and have been deceived by the morning sun's embrace.
It's the right moment to be with a lover…
that is, if I had one;
my last…she dances with somebody else now.
After all options were weighed,
I decided to go for a walk,
to search for some peace of mind (or a cheap thrill).
Nightfall has quickly enveloped the city,
the streetlamps are now on, the moon is set;
the lunatics and novice hookers have started their parade.
The strata of society overlap,
forming human Venn diagrams
made of Brooks Brothers and patched-up hand-me-downs.
It's Friday night
and lust is in the air,
mixed with cologne, perfume and rum vapors.
I seize my place at the bar,
order a beer and shot
and wait for destiny to tap me on the shoulder.

THE FURTHEST THINGS FROM ME

Last night, I lied to myself
when I mused that I was above it all,
when in fact,
I am deeply submerged in it.

It being the hypocrisy of life
that feigns to be two opposite faces
dueling under the same mask,
when it is just an ego-stroke.

Maybe it is sex deprivation,
a way to console myself
when healing shoulders and healing arms
are the furthest things away from me.

The Nihilist Rhapsodizes

A nihilist might say that looking for love
is like looking for the seven lost cities of gold.
That it is a flight of fancy,
like a nymph dancing in a surreal landscape.
"Fuck surrealism! It dies when you realize
that you could no longer escape from yourself."
"And love," the nihilist rhapsodizes,
"is an emotional figment one wishes to be real."
The path to love is littered with casualties,
that is a given.
The object of affection and the rejected become "friends",
the type that will drift away, apart, then back to being strangers.
Love letters, torn and torn again,
are scattered throughout.
Jilted poets sit and sulk at the café,
writhing in their skin that suddenly feels dirty.
Broken-hearted troubadours sadly play their guitars,
hoping to strum away their melancholy.
A lonely romantic sits alone, looking at his wristwatch,
slowly realizing that his time might have passed.
The nihilist laughs at all of them,
but his laughter has a bit of nervousness.
He rushes out the door, but why?
He saw himself in every single one of them.

Sweet Lady Añejo: a Valentine

I stare at my third tumbler full of tequila,
looking at it like I did the other two,
with reverence at this golden,
earth-bound ambrosia,
aged a year or more in old whiskey barrels.
I stare at it like I stare
at the most beautiful women in the world,
while my friends see a whore in clear heels.
My friends' bodies shudder, convulse
at the first whiff of this agave elixir,
as many nights of drunken lapses of judgment
                              all come back, all at once.
My body shudders in ecstasy
every time the first sip
leaves the tumbler
and touches my lip like a kiss
from an angel with gilded wings.
I feel bliss,
I feel closer to nirvana
than my feet feel closer
to the chipped floor.
Sweet lady añejo has never done me wrong,
and she's all right by me.

THE CONSOLER IN SEARCH OF A SYMPATHETIC EAR
(OR: A FLICKERING LIGHT AND AN UNMADE, TWIN-SIZED BED)

I lay my head on my hands,
my fingers, tracing the contours
of the throbbing veins of my temples.
Resignation, regret,
consequences of the night before,
or the ramifications of choices (foolish in nature)
that were made years ago.
The burden seems heavy,
enough to tear Atlas' shoulders
from their sockets.

My body is spread across
an unmade, twin-sized bed.
The wrinkled linen
and comforter-as-pillow
are manifestations
of how messy things are
deep inside my rapidly-fraying core.
There is a flickering light that is on;
I wonder if redemption is on the other side,
or if I forgot to turn off the switch?

I haven't felt this way
since the last woman I genuinely loved
said goodbye.
This feeling… it's like the consoler
in search of a sympathetic ear that is not his own.

Yet, the world seems to be feigning deafness,
or, one voice loudly talking over another—
loud enough to drown me out.

The sun is breaking, the light is still flickering
I have been at this for a while…

If there is an upside to my internal angst,
it's in my ability to telegraph
the personal tribulations of others.
Maybe the answers I have for them
are perfectly suited for me as well.
We all have our moments as prophets
so that we may be absolved
from our moments as fools.
Time will tell if that is so,
or if the flickering light leads me down another rabbit hole.

A SIREN SONG AND ITS INSURMOUNTABLE DISTANCE

My eyes are adrift in a sea
of smog, exhaust and women
with tunnel vision.
Focused on their destination,
they have no time for a casual smile,
or the cat-calls from the undesirables.
But their perfume, their collective perfume-
Opium, Angel, Coco Mademoiselle-
beckons me like a siren song.
And that song…
its echoes and reverberations
sound distant, an insurmountable distance.
A distance where love becomes a memory,
memory becomes a dream,
a dream becomes nothingness.
I fall back into my usual habits
because they are extensions of me
and they are all I have at this moment.
Redundancy is routine,
a rut disguised as comfort
(complacency is apathy?)
Life seems to be
 like a poorly-told joke—
easily telegraphed.
And mine?
It seems to be like a poorly-told joke,
told over and over.

REFRACTION

I stare at the mirror,
for a solid thirty minutes,
I stare.

Why?
I have the slightest idea,
yet, my eyes are transfixed.

Maybe I see
time passing me by
with each new grey hair,

or with the bags
under each one of my eyes
(darker, more sunk in.)

The reflection is growing duller,
more anachronistic,
more futile.

I splash water on my face,
brush my teeth
and shave my alleged beard

(minus the goatee
and sideburns—
it is my signifier.)

It is time to step out
and tenuously hold on
to my ever-fleeting life.

I stare once again,
a quick glance;
my reflection is now
sepia-drenched.

SOLIPSISTIC

I am a caffeine junky
that sits alone
at the patio of a café,
in a silence occasionally broken
by the writhing and spasmodic fit
of a body that wants to
jump and shout in a way
familiar with Methodists
and snake-handling Christians.
On my second cup,
I am sipping it gently,
uttering to myself,
"I like my coffee like I like my women—nerve-fraying."
(My nerves are starting to resemble
the cuffs of my well-worn blazer.)
On my third cup,
the sips are more frequent;
the hands, more jittery.
I start to think about time,
how it passes people by,
how the hours overlap the minutes,
leaving the seconds behind to eat dust.
A fourth cup beckons me,
but the mind is in overdrive,
going at a million thoughts per minute,
thoughts that are jagged, disjointed--
a stream of consciousness
barely contained by puckered lips
and self-awareness.

Fidgeting, I reach for a cigarette
with a twitchy eye staring to my left,
weary of the same scavengers
with their same refrains
("I ran out of smokes and the stores are closed.")
Today has been hobo-free,
and aside from an occasional
 misanthropic fit,
I really cannot complain.
But my mind, my mind is racing,
racing somewhere,
trying to keep a date
I did not even know I had.

In Vice, I Thrust Myself

Sometimes, I feel more obscure
Than all the Spotify playlists in the indie snob's phone.
Like the ever-fading flyer
(of a band that broke up
three days after the advertised date)
taped on a paint-chipped wall,
I stand, hidden by the white noise
of (seemingly) perfectly-sculpted strangers;
of the boundless aura of my friends;
of the jukebox that never plays my songs.
(There seems to be more Ed Hardy aficionados here;
glass of Red Bull and vodka in one hand,
and a mirror to appreciate themselves in the other.)
Aside from my second shot of whiskey,
the only sensation I am feeling
is the vibrating timbre of my phone.
Nothing to get excited about, though,
it was my cell phone provider reminding me
that a payment is due by week's end.
It is just another random evening
and I am indulging in my vice, in the hopes
that it will lead to a pleasure
beyond my fondness of the drink.
Time to order another round
and to see how the evening will progress.

LIFE, LUST, DEATH AND THE SMITHS

I am consumed
by my fascinations;
the urban blight and decay
that doubles as a playground
for both the iconoclasts and the philistines.
Polar opposites meet in the center,
the neon-light-edged center,
united by lust and despair
over the ephemeral nature of life
and the certainty of death.
The young, sexy and foolish
sing along to "How Soon is Now?"
as if it were their personal anthem.
Dancing with such beer-soaked fervor,
one would think that the second coming is imminent.
The sun will rise and cast its rays
on both the sexed-up and the despondent,
and the closest thing to the rapture
is what is playing on a carefully-curated Spotify playlist
("Sister Savior" to be precise.)

My Other Shoe

The pavement-grey, weathered,
pock-marked with gum-
follows a crooked, uneven path,
circular in its motion.
It is a rather crude impression
of a life both interrupted and rerouted;
the forged path runs deep like a moat.
I look for something new within the familiar,
Something to put the rose-tint back on my lenses,
to refresh my jaded soul and apathetic mind.
With each step forward
it all started to have
a Hanna-Barbera-type of monotonous feel—
everything that's old is never new,
but recycled and re-canned.
I have been around this block before—
same walls (though they've gone from blue to grey);
same cracks on the pavement;
same crumpled pack of generic cigarettes
lying in the gutter.
Nothing has changed…
other than the gum stuck underneath
my other shoe.

Living in a City Named After a Saint

I live in a city named after a saint,
but Eden is a mere speck
in the rearview mirror,
an image that gets more faint
with each mile that's traveled
in a car with balding tires,
or in shoes with holes
worn through near the heel.
Prostitutes that look nothing like the movies
(legitimate or pornographic)
walk past as I sip on a coffee.
The click-clack of their clear-heeled shoes
pass through the street like a reverberation
through an empty room,
or like an old woman
who's the last to enter the cathedral
(everybody turns around).
Part-time hustlers stop
to look at their own reflections on the window.
They stare hard,
as if they are trying to conjure up
an image that is nowhere near
their actual representation.
A disgruntled parking compliance officer
drives and stalks the cars parked in the meter zone,
eyeing each one slowly,
counting backwards to zero;
leniency is a word foreign to him.

The same ties and the same shirts,
the same skirts and the same blouses,
they all seem to walk and talk alike;
they all have tunnel vision-
point A to point B.
Buses zoom past,
the smoke from their exhaust pipes
momentarily turns the air grey...
my white shirt as well.
Time burns slowly,
only my pure-tobacco cigarettes
burn slower.
The faces become familiar,
as it's the second (or third) time they have passed,
the differences?
A jogger asked me for a cigarette,
and a homeless lady sarcastically coughed
as I finished my cigarette
(and my coffee session).

In This Glorified Suburb

A breath is drawn,
slowly,
like a fog that sets down
over the city.

It is more like a sigh,
both of pleasure
and resignation…
another day in this glorified suburb.

Bus rides that lead somewhere,
though this final destination
seems like nowhere.
I feel as if this has already been done.

Coffee and cigarettes,
music and solitude…
Headphones are on,
in search of sonic salvation…

I unfurl the New York Times,
and what happened yesterday
is happening today,
and will happen tomorrow.

Dishonest politicians,
war in perpetuity,
the rise of both the new plutocracy
and of idiot America…

Boy-hungry priests
and meth-addicted Pentecostal pederasts
tell me that I am going to hell
(while they fondle somebody's cock).

Women are my inspiration,
the source of joy and pain,
of simplistic heartbreak
that pretends to be profound.

A breath is drawn...
muffled by my left hand,
while my right is busy
with a lit cigarette.

Time marches on—
and while people change clothes,
jobs and sexual partners,
the news will always be the same.

CONTEMPLATIONS AND TRIVIAL PURSUITS

In the tinderbox that is my room,
I stare at the ceiling
and the rafters holding it in its place.
The day replays in my mind,
the images—now drenched
in sepia tones and lightly scratched.
I think about the phone
and the calls that never came through,
assuring me an open day
for contemplations and trivial pursuits.
I am drinking coffee—
the same way as yesterday,
from the same place,
but the coffee is good,
so there are no complaints from me.
Women I will never have sex with
came and went, occasionally stopping
to readjust their overstuffed redwelds,
or to contemplate a chai latte.
A hobo with shoes nicer than mine
asked me for a couple of dollars
(briefly, I thought about economics,
about how inflation works),
I said no and he looked at me like how a priest
must look at parishioners swimming in lies.
I soon started to think about boxing,
and life resembles the sweet science:
the suits walk around like champions;
delivery drivers behave like contenders;

students are like prospects;
hobos with omnipresent odor
function like professional opponents;
I, on the other hand, feel like a fringe contender—
whose success is sprinkled with setbacks.
In the tinderbox that is my room,
I stare at the ceiling
and the rafters holding it in its place.
I stare as if I am waiting
for something to happen,
or for a non-existent lover
to slide into bed.
But in all honesty,
I am waiting for my body
to succumb to exhaustion.

LIKE AN EBBING TIDE

I walk through the Plaza de César Chávez,
past the Christmas decorations,
the throng of gawkers and idle phone carnies.
The bright lights blink
at a seizure-inducing speed—
on and off, off and on (I stare).
I can not remember how long I was there,
I just know that somewhere between seven and ten songs played
and the sun gave way to the moon.
I am in the ether—
my feet clumsily search for stable ground
in a nebulous atmosphere.
The past and future
swirl and slosh through the present,
making it a murky concept.
Families and lovers come and go
like an ebbing tide,
receding like both the scent of kettle corn and the past.
I remove my headphones
and I look around…
I thought I heard my name.
All I heard was the wind blowing past me,
ricocheting between the walls of English,
Spanish, Vietnamese, Hindi, Samoan and Farsi.
Yet my name was not uttered,
so I go in search of a chance
to hear familiar voices and see familiar faces.
Instead of seeing faces warmer than my pea coat,
I see the same set of indifferent eyes
that only care if I have money to pay for my coffee.

So I walk…
couples rush past me,
as if they're chasing a romance that is trying to evade them.
I get home after a few twists and turns
on the bus taking me to the part of San José
that resembles a dying suburb.
My messenger bag crashing to the floor,
I turn on the lights of my room
and start to look around.
My eyes drift to a photo
of a house that is no longer mine
(my mind drifts to a time that is no longer mine).
Then again, time is never really a possession,
rather, it is borrowed, and slick in nature,
slipping through the fingers and running back to where it came
from.

CHRIST-HUSTLERS AND PLEASURE-SEEKERS

With autumn comes shorter days,
and with longer nights,
all that makes downtown repulsive-
yet, charming-are in full nocturnal bloom.
Deviants and degenerates are drawn to the neon lights,
inviting one a cirrhosis-inducing good time.
The down-and-out ask for a dollar, or a cigarette,
or offer a dollar for four cigarettes.
Office dwellers-drinking martinis-talk of immigration control
while salivating over the young Mexican female flower vendor in tran-
sit.
Suburban, ghettoized teens act like fools
while one-time barrio natives talk of mergers and acquisitions.
Christ-hustlers thump their bibles and speak of the end-of-days,
and pleasure-seekers
dance in between the soapbox pulpit and the bar:
hymns of Christ and rhythmic hedonism mix like fire and ice.
I walk alone, amongst this pastiche of humanity,
doing my fair-share of head-shaking and sympathizing,
all the while, a disheveled old homeless man yells at none and all,
"What the fuck do you all know about me!?!"

WE WALK ALONG THE GUTTER

We walk along the gutter,
following a floating cigarette pack.
Our feet slosh through the runoff,
wetting the soles of our shoes.
It is Thursday night,
we are going from place to place,
each location gets hazier and hazier,
the drinks, stronger and more potent.
We hold hands and laugh,
it is the time of our lives,
even the smoke of our cigarettes
playfully mingle with one and other.
Tonight, I am all about you,
my body shudders when you run your finger
over my tattoos, over the logo
of my Love and Rockets t-shirt.
Tonight, you are all about me,
as I stare into your eyes
and play with your hair
(how it looks like Bette Davis' in "All About Eve").
Without knowing, we turn the corner,
passing the Greyhound station,
the bustle and the idleness is much like life
(stop and go; going everywhere and nowhere, all at once.)
The vintage sounds of Manchester
can be heard from behind the black curtain,
the outside of the club is teeming
with chain-smoking hipsters.
We heed the siren's call and make our way in,
and after one shot each of Jägermeister,
we make our way to the floor, to dance our way into a singular unit.

WE RUN LIKE THIEVES

We run like thieves,
we hide in the shadows
and from one and other.
We feel guilty,
like catholic sinners
and regretful lovers.
We rue the night we mixed,
long after the pleasure elapsed;
we proved its transient value.
We blame the alcohol,
we blame it for finding
and igniting our suppressed urges.
We blame the weather
for driving us to find shelter
within each other's arms.
It is morning now,
but I am pretty sure it's midnight somewhere,
so, we run...

...His Pale Horse Gallops Slowly

Lovers amble on; hands gripped tightly,
not wanting to let go of an already fleeting moment.
Is it bliss or myopia?
Both tangle underneath the same mask.
I light a cigarette and smile...
at how we think forever is ours.
Transience is the lone constant of existence:
Fashion and opinions; how often do they change?
Today will be tomorrow
and yesterday will be obsolete
(relevant only in the mind
when one indulges in nostalgia).
What is life if not a series of temporal moments?
Midway though my cigarette,
three sisters-in-Christ approach,
handing me a flier trumpeting
the eventual arrival of the rapture
(not the "House of Jealous Lovers" singers).
"Repent, or perish!
Save yourself now, eternal salvation awaits."
For the first time ever,
the words "you are going to hell"
had a seductive tone to them.
Transience is the lone constant of existence;
Today will be tomorrow
and yesterday will be obsolete.
Nothing lasts forever;
not this cigarette, not this life.
Nothing else to do
but to smoke, drink and wait for death
(his pale horse gallops slowly).

A Meditation on Death (RIP Abuelita María)

We as humans have always been scared of death. It is a concept we try to compartmentalize in the furthest recess of our minds; as evidence by the color it was assigned...black. Its skeletal representation further conveys the ominous tone of inevitability. Some cultures fear it more than others, but fear it nonetheless. Even Mexicans-who dance and mock death in a manner the late Octavio Paz has written about-fear it once it comes to collect its toll. We can zig- zag to and fro; we can exercise and eat vegan; we can take as many supplements as we can, all it will do is push us to the back of the line. Death reminds us that at the end, we are more servant than master.

Why am I meditating on death-the ghoulish and harshest of subjects? I would like to say that it is nothing more than a morbid and macabre flight of fancy, but that would be a lie. It would be nobler of me to say that it is of concern over what is going on in all corners of the world, but it would only be partially true. As I visited my grandmother, who is recuperating at White Blossom Convalescent (nursing/old folks) Home from a fall she had, I just started thinking about death as that omnipresent soul collector, whose visage is clothed in black. Though she seems to be getting better, at times it feels as if he's knocking on her door. I take a break to go have a cigarette. Stepping out of her room and snaking through corridors like a sterilized maze, I notice the other residents (mostly elders at various stages of finality; some with visitors, some alone). Outside are shrubs and poinsettias; I nearly feel guilty about my need to light up, but I did.

I took a long drag and started to think about all this (fixing the "visitor" sticker that seems to be peeling off of my sweater vest). I take another drag, pointing out to myself the irony about the thought of death and my concern of it. We all have vices, and I am aware that what I am doing could quite possibly upgrade my own ticket from coach to first-class. All of that is cast aside as I notice a family getting out of a sedan, making their way through the door. I wonder which elderly resident will be really happy to see them and which elderly resident will look despondent and lament another lonely day. Putting out my cigarette, the automatic sprinklers turned on, soaking me as I tried to get out of the way.

I went back inside to see if my abuelita needed anything. She said that she was okay. In the room was my mother, my father, my aunt Filomena and my grandmother's roommate, a Tejana named Eugenia. Walking in, death was the topic of discussion. In Spanish, my dad said, "I went to Redwood City the other day to visit some friends of mine from back home (Aguillia, Michoacán, México). Once there, I went to Artemio Gómez's apartment, his son answered the door and said 'Don Pedro, my dad passed away three days ago. We're making arraignments to ship his body back to México.' I stayed for a few minutes to give my condolences and then I said that I was going to go see if Lorenzo Mata was at his place, since I haven't seen or spoken to him in a few months. 'Don Pedro,' Artemio's son continued, 'Lorenzo passed away as well. He died a week before my dad's passing.'" Looking rather reflective, my dad continued, "that's two friends that went, and I am older than they were. I remember when we were all back in México…" My dad trailed off, his voice turned to an inaudible mutter, his old-world machismo stifling his need to cry; everyone in the room nodded and turned to the television (Sábado Gigante is on). It seems as if I am not the only one that can feel death's presence in this place. I am not the only that notices how it lingers here like a specter, biding its time.

It was thirty minutes passed nine on this Saturday evening; a nurse came by to remind us that it was time for us to go. My grandmother looked a little bit sad, but she never goes a day without at least one family member coming for a visit. Eugenia spoke Spanish and was friendly to my grand mother, talking to her daily. We all said our goodbyes and promised to bring her some "real food" (i.e. comida mexicana). The halls are empty now, save for one doctor and the late shift nurses and orderlies making their rounds, doing what they can to make things pleasant (and yes, fool death for another night). My aunt went to her car, saying goodbye to us; we returned the gesture in kind. I got into the back seat of the car (before that, I was counting the random number of "visitor" stickers thrown about the parking lot), my mom and dad were outside debating as to who would drive back home (neither of them wanted to do so). I looked back and stared at the doors of this place. White Blossom Convalescent Home is a name that should conjure up a vision so calm and serene that the transition would be seamless and fluid. The closest one can come to St. Peter and the gates he mans, while on earth, would be the doors to a convalescent home.

LIFE (AS LIVED THROUGH PULP'S "COMMON PEOPLE")

The sun sets slowly,
as if it's held captive
by the never-ending cavalcade
of cars rushing to the nearest on-ramp.
Sugar packets mingle with fallen leaves
over the coffee-stained pavement
(I wonder how many times
absent-minded office workers curse themselves
while looking at their now-off-white oxford shirt…)
I stare at my Vans-
specifically at the slowly-expanding rupture
taking shape on my right shoe.
The occasional errant leaf
is a reminder that nature is losing the battle
as towns rush to become metropolitan.
There is life in these streets,
maybe not mine,
but there is life nonetheless,
as evidenced by a shadow here and there,
being dragged to somewhere it doesn't want to be.
At times, I don't know where I want to be,
living life, as Jarvis Cocker once sang,
"With no meaning or control/With nowhere else to go."
Perhaps, that is why we emulate zombies,
devoid of any purpose,
except, I walk with jittery hands…
once again, I had way too much coffee today.

WAX RHAPSODIC

It's a semi-splendid day;
sunny, but cloudy-
raindrops on the verge of falling.
Downtown never changes,
it resembles an Eden
teetering on the edge of its expiration date.
Boarded-up windows
represent dreams born and dead
on the whim of others.
What is life if not
a mixture of hard luck
and self-chosen fate?
From a hole-in-a-wall,
echoes drift in and out,
while the collective sound of the jukebox,
the clashing billiard balls
and the never-idle beer tap
mingle with the smoke of a hand-rolled cigarette
the man with the ever-changing face
is smoking outside.
Random groups of threes and twos
 (and sometimes one)
are randomly strewn around
the dimly-lit tavern,
exchanging nods of the head
and stories of a brighter yesterday.
Street preachers stand in the center
of the promenade
bustling with lunch-hour traffic,
(spasmodically) preaching about love in one hand

and condemnation on the other,
picking and choosing
verses to fit their perspective.
The more he is ignored,
the more spasmodic he becomes,
until a female college student
comes and flashes her breast in front of him.
In shock, he packed up and left.
Nothing happens by Providence…
or does it?
The semi-splendid day
has come and gone.
Will tomorrow be another story,
or will serendipity bring everyone together
for round two?

THAT IS WHY WE SING THE SONGS THAT WE DO

When you are popular and adored,
the world seems to slow down for you
and streetlights seem to be an eternal green.
When you are relegated to the background,
you are nothing more than a bit player
in that badly cast play known as life.
Sometimes I feel alone and lost
like a traveler through a city
that I have known all my life.
The vapid nature
of idle chatter has me
longing for what is rapidly receding.
Head hung low, I hum a song,
eyes squinted, I try to remember
when I heard it last.
It can't be a song on the radio,
since I've eschewed that pre-fab contraption
that feels like a minstrel show in a constant loop.
Maybe it was a song my Mother sang to me,
of a México cherished and adored,
rapidly becoming a myth in my shifting memories.
Maybe it was a fly-by-night indie smash,
that momentarily amuses the ears,
only to flee at the first sign of light.
I struggle to remember if I heard an accordion,
or if it was a Moog synthesizer
cascading over a reverb-drenched guitar riff.
The consumption this song has brought
has me forgetting that I am a bit player
in the life outside.

Rather, through a disaffected disposition,
I feel a semblance of control,
even if the lights are more red than green.
Head is no longer hung low,
the provenance of one's despair does not matter
when you feel a sense of control.
That is why we sing the songs that we do,
to remember what made us laugh and cry,
to remember our roots (even if they feel like phantom limbs).

I Am That Piece of Creased Paper

I am that piece of creased paper
that drifts between your liberal guilt
and conservative reaction.
Drifting like a vagabond
with no purpose or aim,
other than to drift forward, sideways
and onward once again.
The man pushing the cart
full of smashed cans
has direction.
The woman standing at the corner,
waving a cardboard arrow
is giving directions.
Me, I walk around long city blocks,
staring at the sun like a newly-freed convict
getting a whiff of smog-tinged freedom.
There are decisions to be made,
but all I see are rhetorical roundabouts,
and the end is the beginning.
There's an end-times preacher
convulsing at the sight of two homosexuals
holding hands.
I smear a ketchup packet (that I somehow have)
in the center of my hands
and ran-a-shrieking across him…
screaming, "bloody miracle!"
Walking around the bend,
I see a flock of Pigeons,
and I start to think of how people
love to pigeon-hole one and all.

I start to think even further back,
at the times that both my Mexican-American--
and East Side credentials--
were called into question.
To be a full tribesman of one or the other,
there are certain catalogs one must subscribe to,
otherwise you are white-washed—
a marginal sort outside of the margins.
I might be white-washed,
but they are the ones living life
 like the Man's perception
of what it is to be a stock-footage minority.

"ALTERNAVERSE"

Art is more like commerce,
a trafficked commodity
lorded over by bearded chin-strokers
and erstwhile muses-turned-cynical pixie hausfraus.
Politics and glad-handing
have replaced merit and genuine discovery.
If one's name has any currency,
the doors open wide,
but if your name is something you
can't even barter, well, good luck.
A gaggle of intentional-slackers
dot the bar like pigs at a trough
drinking Pabst Blue Ribbon,
making snide remarks
to mask the bitterness of both the beer
and how no matter how hard they try,
their look could never be more than intentional.

(You have to be an individual,
just like everybody else in this two-bit bar.)

In this alternaverse,
the revolution will be televised,
dressed in Ché Guevara shirts
and dreadlocks (or at the very least,
looking like a roadie for Iron and Wine),
both hidden by a made-in-China
zip-up hooded sweater.
Rebellion was never free-range,
more like cattle and prisoners;

manned watchtowers dot the corners,
high above the grazing denizens,
and freedom is when one is deemed "cool".
Art is more like commerce,
and whatever song or author you hold dear,
you can be rest assured that
you are not the only one enjoying the sad strains,
or the melancholic prose.

Alas (Another Day Has Started)

Buzz... *buzz*... BUZZ goes the alarm;
another day has started,
another day I start with a curse-word or two.
My eyes half-open, my body shakes in denial,
already projecting how this day will end
(with a Y, always with a Y... sometimes, with a why).
In the race to the beginning I beat the sun,
but it is a race I did not volunteer for,
the alarm was set at the wrong time.
To say that it is dark outside
is to say that all of Mazzy Star's songs are sad;
it is a given.
The sun rises slowly,
moving like a stalker through the bushes,
waiting for its moment to (not really) surprise us all.
Defeated, I head for the shower
to wash off the dirt
and any remaining temptation to head back to bed.
With my head underneath the nozzle,
I found myself briefly envying the comatose,
at least, the perceived sense of their serenity,
but that's when the hot water started to run out.
Rinsed off, dressed and satchel packed,
I head to the kitchen,
the first thing I see is a tall can of Yuban
and a coffee maker that has not been used
since the Clinton administration
(I wonder if there's a line that connects these dots).
Walking out the door,
I queue-up Shugo Tokumaru's "Parachute"

in the hopes that its Sufjan Stevens-like melodies
in sync with the giddy optimism
that only seems to come from Japan
will help me start off on the right foot.
So far, it seems to be working.
The sun seems to be swaying to its own beat,
which seems to be to the chime
of a jack-in-a-box.
I briefly look at the timestamp on my iPod,
it informs me that it is 8:30 am...
fuck it's early, I don't have to be at work until 4 o'clock,
but I did beat the sun, and that was a victory,
unwanted or otherwise.
Here comes the 22,
the proletariats' limousine
(and from 11:00pm to now, a mobile homeless motel).
The ride is a bumpy one,
and the air that is circulated inside
has the taste of unwashed bodies.
(Right now, "I Touch Roses" by Book of Love is playing;
though I know the song is about female masturbation,
I take it to be literal, in light of my surroundings.)
 I am at the first leg of my destination—First and Santa Clara:
the sun shines on both the self-talking bearded fellow
with a predilection for outdoor urination
and the self-respected business folk
(with secret lovers and secret drug habits) that avoid him.
I make a b-line towards my favorite morning caffè
to get my cup of legalized meth,
with two shots of espresso and hazelnut syrup.

I have already had two cigarettes,
but they were prologue to the one I am having now,
the true first cigarette of the day,
the one had after two sips of some strong drip.
The feeling that I am experiencing…
it is as if the caffeine and the nicotine are in mid-coitus
while I stare off into the wilderness of tall buildings
and a street that is currently doubling as a parking lot.
People are walking through,
doing a spot-on impression of a Montana cattle drive.
I am currently stuck on my third crossword puzzle;
surprise surprise, it is from the New York Times,
it is mocking me with what I believe it to be
a snide, Upper East Side old-money accent.
Slowly but surely, I was conquering it,
one letter at a time
and one huge cigarette and coffee binge.
I thrust my fist in the air,
in a geeky glee.
As if the day couldn't get any better,
I got a call from a girl that semi-likes me.
She said to meet her at 12:00pm
over at the Farmer's Market.
I know I shouldn't take comfort in her semi-liking me
since there is room for "not really",
but she wants to have lunch,
and who am I to say no to that?

ROBERTO BOLAÑO

You are the link
between Bukowski, Kerouac
and my reflection in the mirror.
Your travails through Mexico City
and the old continent
spoke to me in earnest,
giving a voice to the gutter rats
and the street vendors
while others spoke of the intangible.
So vivid were your words,
I could see the cigarette smoke
mingling with the humming neon lights
of red light districts.
The pen and your mind
made cerebral love,
giving birth to your visceral realism.
The light you have shone
shines still within me
(it runs through me like a Savage Detective[s]).

THE SHAKY CONVICTIONS OF THE EASILY AMUSED

Monday morning:
the traffic lights only seem
to be going from yellow to red--
cars are bumper to bumper,
giving birth to smog and anxiety.
Everybody's destination seems to be distant,
distant like the idle gods above.
I have no place to be,
so urgency is far from what I am feeling.
Off the path, a castle of a basilica
can be seen from a distance-
tenderly woven into the tapestry
of office buildings and half-empty condo units.
Its bells dance and play with the wailing sirens
of a speeding police cruiser.
A surly priest can be heard lamenting
over former parishioners, how they
walked into the dark side that is Protestantism.
In modern times, tenets are only as firm
as the shaky convictions of the easily amused.
The faith of my Fathers is thrust onto me-
and that religion replaced religions-
by the sheer virtue of my birth.
Though baptized, it felt as if
there was no indoctrination, no rite,
just a book full of arcane prose
passed down by generations
(and through a now-fortified border)
and a sense of instilled shame:
I search for redemption,
not knowing what I did.

ACKNOWLEDGMENTS

Where would I be if it weren't for the people in my life— those who are present and those who are memories set in amber? For my dad, you loved me in the only way you knew, which I learned to appreciate later on in life. To my siblings, we weren't the Brady Bunch, but we loved each other all the same. To William Botero, my cousin who is still like a twin, born six months apart. Salvador Rangel and Molly Vásquez, two constant presences in this ephemeral world of ours. "La Cuatro," the times we've had are forever ours—The Talking Torta can attest. Martin, "Yoshi," Paolo, José Prado, Val—both sides of King Road were the good sides. Michael "DJ Basura" Boado, you have set the soundtrack to the halcyon days of my life. Javier, Chris, Kate, Mike, and the regulars at the late Cinebar —"The Sinner" lives on, even if the building doesn't (RIP Jesus). Ms. Heffley (RIP), you would have liked to have thumbed through the pages that bear my name. Diego García (ex-Elefant), I wish the band would put out one more album.

ABOUT THE AUTHOR

José-Ariel Cuevas is a lifelong independent scholar, forever in pursuit of knowledge, with his head in the clouds and his proletariat feet firmly planted on the ground. Rooted in a deep commitment to critical thought and social consciousness, he navigates the world with an insatiable curiosity, bridging the realms of theory and lived experience. His writings have been published in *Eastside Magazine*, where he became the first poet to take the leap, setting the stage for countless other poets to add their voices to the publication. Whether immersed in books or engaged in dialogue, José-Ariel approaches learning as a lifelong journey—one that is both intellectual and grounded in the realities of everyday life.

www.ingramcontent.com/pod-product-compliance
Lightning Source LLC
Chambersburg PA
CBHW010939120626
46554CB00008B/2538